MW01287306

How to Get a Man that Doesn't Cheat

by
Charles E. Hughes

authorHOUSE™

1663 LIBERTY DRIVE, SUITE 200
BLOOMINGTON, INDIANA 47403
(800) 839-8640
WWW.AUTHORHOUSE.COM

First published by AuthorHouse 10/20/2005

ISBN: 1-4208-7591-4 (sc)

Printed in the United States of America
Bloomington, Indiana

This book is printed on acid-free paper.

This book is written to help women enter a world that no one thought is possible. This book can and will give hope to the hopeless. If you are truly looking for a real man, you could be enlighten in these truths; not just facts, opinions or false knowledge.

Chapter 1

Built to be a Non-cheating Man

A man that does not cheat is the gold-find that most women seem to want. This type of man can be built, and he does exist. I was born in Queens, New York, named Charles Edward Hughes, Jr. As I grew up I began to realize how special my name was. I did not know what my name meant, but I knew that who I was named after was relevant to who I must act like and become. This was my foundation for who I am today. I am a non-cheating man. This is not because I say so, I could be a liar.

Please do not think that I am righteous, because I am not. I hate religion. You say, "but I thought you were a Christian?" I am. A true Christian is not religious. Religion is evil (back to this later). Christianity is relationship, not religion with God.

Do you notice that when someone teaches you something, and you succeed at it, and it benefits you, that usually that person you learned from knows his or her "stuff". Well, I will show you that I know my "stuff". I am a non-cheating "expert", since that word might give me some respect. Just to let you know, I really do not believe experts, and you shouldn't, but if it is positive, try their advice.

When something is positive, it heals for the long run, it helps you now and in the long-run. Would you not agree that positivity means going higher, better, "truer" and brighter.

The reason that I said this chapter is named "Built to be a Non-Cheating Man", is because I was "built that way". The way a diamond if formed from coal. This expression though is ironic: because a diamond is built under pressure. I had no pressure, believe it or not. But, as a diamond comes from coal, I came from my parent's relationship.

My parent's relationship was great, but as you know, great relationships can go bad. Theirs did not; I said they could go bad because other great relationships have.

They were and are married over thirty-two years. Other relationships have had this great longevity, and still break-ups occur.

Why do I state positive "trues" and yet there are some negative occurrences that still occurs? This is because of the "missing ingredients" of the spiritual world. What am I talking about?

I am talking about building. Any relationship can look or seem good on the outside, like wood or fruit that looks good and not good within. You may say "but you can see wood start to rot, or a fruit turn bad". You know what I am going to say, so I'll say it.

Bad things start inside before they manifest outside. (Real is unseen, unreal is seen). Back to this later. Just remember this truth, -spirit then mind then body, unseen then seen.

This "missing ingredient" I said before from the spirit world is the very ingredient, the very thing that is missing in relationships. It is called what it is "missing ingredient" (for now).

It's the plus in an A+, it's the 10 in 110%, and it's the unexpecting hope that is easily not seen, and yet easy to be seen. (Weirdness, I know), but these things will unfold, keep reading.

Back to the situation from before, my parents, they were just different. They were odd. They were special, I basically seen how they acted and read between the lines. They acted in ways that you may say are not possible, how could they, how could I be like that? It doesn't matter about every detail of their lives; I am the way I am from them.

By my mother, I never was told not to cheat, or should I say I was never told. She was a person who did not have the friends people had. What do I mean? My mother, I cannot remember seeing with any friends. She took me to and from school, etc. etc. What does this have to do with the subject? (Hold on please, I'm getting there).

By my father, I was never told not to cheat. Him, I also never seen with friends. But, he would come straight home after work. What does this mean?

This means that their ways are in me (I know that's obvious, what else you say), also, something about this relates to not being a cheater.

Somehow these missing-friends seemed to help built a relationship with them not cheating on each other and it is in me.

I know I either lost you or you probably think I am implying that one cannot have friends; I am not implying this.

By my parents not having friends, I (simply-thinking) think it helped them focus on each other. I definitely do not think this is all that helped them-not cheat, but no one can persuade me that it hurt them being together.

I was not told I couldn't have friends, decades ago I had the amount of friends you can count on one hand. But today, I do not really have friends, (visiting friend-friends). I believe I like people, but I just do not make the effort to invite over, and I do not go and visit.

Why are we this way? Why are we odd like this? I really cannot explain, I am tempted to just say I know not or I don't know (but this would be a lie). I believe I know and the answer is, "God made me this way". You see, this phrase is overused, but it's the only one I can think of (right now), without creating another book. But I will tell you, God does not make anything negative, or that does not make sense. What you do not understand now, you will understand later, if it's godly, (keep reading). Whatever is ungodly will be misunderstood forever, even when trying to understand, (there I go again). Let me open up to you (a little) right now, (more later)...but.

When I wrote these things you have just read in this chapter, I do not write thinking I am better than you. I write these "trues" to make you better.

I am overly humble and too self critical at times. So critical, that I used to keep my mouth shut about relationships. I know I always had what it takes to get the truth out, but I had no boldness.

Now I stand in boldness, and go that extra mile by "going" that mile. The mile that I was not used to. The mile-never ran. I now run this mile for the women of the world.

On a more (developed-thinking) level, on a deeper-thinking level as opposed to my first stated (simply-thinking), I do not cheat because my parents (especially father) doesn't cheat. This does not prove anything, I know, but just keep reading, (I will not say this phrase again.)

As you find out and see more of me in my writing, you will see that truth and ways of truth will come out, and you can judge for yourself.

This chapter was to be about foundations. As best I tried to express, it will all come together. Foundations never seem like much. You never see the final result yet. But, everything lies upon the foundation. Good foundations last, no matter how they seem, understanding them or not.

A foundation in anything must be pure. If it is to be mixed, mix it with the necessary ingredients.

No one should be around when a foundation is being created, except the proper builders.

In the next chapters, truth will shine bright that no one really had seen before. The truth was always there but no one has reason to "see" it.

Open your mind and "look for the stars at dusk or dawn". Reading this book is like seeking the moon in the day. Giving a dollar to a homeless person. What I mean is going the extra mile to see something that is there, or that helping someone means something.

Change is love, when changing for the better; but yet love never changes. Love never changes for worst. You see, what means and makes sense, and sometimes little "non-sense" makes all the sense in some of the world.

Chapter 2

What a Non-cheating man is made of

A non-cheating man is not just a man, but a real man. A real man does not cheat. Let me explain. Think; boys cheat (whether in school or even on taxes), they cheat: not men who are real. A "boy" is someone up in age who is male that does wrong and knows it.

A male child is a boy and a man can act like a boy. A boy causes trouble to someone who is older and or more mature (not necessarily older).

Naturally women are more mature, and none of this is male bashing. It is not that they are "more mature", but they can accept being wrong: quicker than a man. I did not say a real man, I said a man.

A mature person can accept wrong, and be corrected. The kind of "wrong-ness" I am speaking about is that annoying troubling "wrong-ness", in relation-ships.

Who is usually right, it's the woman. You see, this world is contaminated with lies and anti-relationship -cynical thinking. So everything is backwards and different thoughts can attack any persons mind.

It is usually the men who are attacked in their minds and do not even know it. They are supposed to be the head and their thinking is "my way or no way". I hate to have to talk on good and evil so soon but; all thinking comes from good (positive or fair) and (negative) evil and or lies.

This negative or hypocritical thinking, or whatever is unfair or bad; gets in the mans head the most. The "negative forces" know that he is suppose to lead, and if his thinking is messed up so will the woman's, and (there goes the family-hood).

Women have negative thoughts too, but they usually don't initially make the relationship take a turn for the worst. She can keep her bad thoughts to herself, usually. It is usually him or both or if it's just her, some "head" headed her this way.

A real man is beyond this. From the beginning of a relationship, you can notice that some signs are less arguing, and much more easiness of hearing and listening.

There is lack of sexual pressure. More opening-up of himself and lack of male friends (when you are around).

You see, my father taught me about being a real man by teaching me about the masculine mind and the feminine mind.

These mentalities are not only associated with a male or female body. Anyone can have a masculine or feminine mind. I will explain [(and by the way) a real man (a non-cheating man) can explain as opposed to excuses, most of the time].

A real man has a masculine mind, which means he is positive. He gives. A real man always gives. The only taking a real man should do is in taking wisdom and knowledge in and of Godliness; taking advice, positively adding to his character.

A real man's thinking is admitting error. Remember this world is anti-relationship, pro-fighting, pro-divorce, and pro-splitting up. So when a man is doing or thinking wrong, he has a normal thinking mind, (a worldly mind).

This kind of mind is a feminine mind. Remember, it is not about gender when it comes to the mind; its masculine or feminine. "Good or evil", when it comes to the mind.

A feminine mind is an evil mind, (I did not say a female is evil). This is all mental. When a person (especially) a man has a feminine mind, this means he takes any negative advice that the world or his "boys" or his "dudes" give him.

Taking in good is not evil, in-taking evil or wrong or unfairness is evil.

An example of a masculine and feminine mind is this: "John" has a girl friend: "John" is with his girl a month. "John's" friends call him to a party. The masculine thinking John would intake good advice (past or present). He would take his girlfriend or say he doesn't want to go. He could even go without her, if they both agreed. This is positive, positive, and neutral.

As a pro-relationship person (in the name of this book, in the spirit of this book) the positive thing to do was bring his girl or not go. I call his going with out her neutral, because I am not seeing how he could be with his friends and not her. Why would he want to go without her, or what (in this young-time-wise relationship) could cause her to agree to not go with him.

It wasn't any business or work related situation stopping them from being together. No funeral, no one sick; that's why it's neutral to me- neither positive or negative, mentality-wise.

This may seem small, to a man or woman, but not a real man or real woman: and we are discussing real men right now.

Now, the feminine thinking man, would go without her right away. "John" would not see the importance of taking her. His friends would say, "why she has to come", "you been with her a month", or, "don't tell her".

John would be taking negative advice. Taking negative means evil, pain-causing to self or others-kind of advice. Selfish, me-me-me advice. World advice. She is a "ball-and-chain" advice.

The masculine mind gives advice that can also be given again. The feminine mind takes advice that is negative, and can cause pain, mistrust, angry feelings and sadness.

Let me go to that spirit world and pullout another good one. [(When I say spirit world, I am trying to keep from preaching (obviously, for now)] I am keeping it indirect for now. Indirectly, meaning I'll keep it labeled good advice (not negative) advice from the spirit world.

A masculine mind is strong and made up. He does not fall for the common feelings that regular men act out. (notice I said act out). Negativity attempts to enter any mindset, but a masculine mind rejects those negative, boyish thoughts (evil), (taking-thoughts). He gives like God gives. Like a masculine body-organ "physically" gives, and gives seed, if chosen to do so.

A feminine mind takes like a feminine body-organ takes-in. A feminine mind takes any negative advice. The advice that takes relationships, lives, time, and values.

I have to go there: the devil takes and good-God gives.

Pain, waste, lying, hypocrisy, envy, and anything negative takes, (which is of the devil).

Once again, a female is not evil, neither is her precious feminine body-organ. This is speaking in terms of nature. One has to give and one has to receive, in nature (physically).

On a mental level, a strong mind takes good advice, (in actuality, one can not even take good, they actually add it on to themselves. "Take" is a figure of speech, when you take good, you become it. Positivity adds to itself even when it gives. Negativity takes, and destroys and kills.

When a woman takes, it is not evil, because a taker should have a giver; so things can be balanced. Give and take should be physical, and if it's mental it's receiving positive or negative thinking. Positive goes to happiness to life to love. Negativity goes to no-peace, fights, stubbornness, lying, etc.

Remember, early in the book, I said lets go to a world thought not possible to go to. Well, if you got pass the last bunch of sentences, just listen to this. This is boldness on "paper". This will be loved by women and hated by men. Loved by women who are real and loved by men who are real men. (Remember I said, I am writing not to show that I am better than any woman, or any man, but I want the reader to be better, and have better).

Men readers who will read what I'm about to write will hate it, real men will love it or at least understand that I mean well.

A man should always pay. What? I said a man should always pay. Why? Is this my opinion? Well, it's my book I can easily say yes, but my opinion does not matter. You know what it is anyway, if you are a real man or real woman.

Most men will not be reading this book. But, to you ladies, I really want you to get a good man that doesn't cheat, and believe me; this paying subject has something to do with it. These truths are signs you women could use to find a good man, a real man, a non-cheating man. It's all related. Yes, and hard to swallow.

You see, God made a man, and anything God made the devil tries to mess with. (You see God and the devil are coming out of me in this book). It's not that I don't like to write about God and the devil, I just do not want this book to be labeled religious. The word religious scares people away. Once again, I am not religious. God isn't either. So readers keep reading. I hate religion. (hate- a figure of speech). Religion is evil.

Now back to the paying subject. God made man to hunt, bring food, give, etc. You know the story. When a man pays, it is like he has hunted, and he is bringing home food. [(Remember, when good advice is given, then evil (negative) advice tries to come right in)]; example: "But hey, the man didn't really hunt, the food was cooked, and that woman he is paying for did not even cook it." Well, thank you "negativity" for your observation.

When a person is nature-minded, he will see things naturally (obviously), but, when he is spiritual, he will see things spiritually (unnatural-not making sense), or maybe one does not want to make the sense of it. (notice: another spiritual truth- senses are selfish- they see and hear what they see and hear, they never go that extra mile and really see or hear).

Women are you learning, are you seeing and hearing, rightly.

Do not argue with a man, this is a bad sign (in a beginning relationship). Remember your goal, to have a man that does not cheat. Everything relates back to if he would cheat or not.

I will be called crazy, for all of this, but I wasn't crazy before I wrote this book: and, by the way, any right or righteousness will be attacked. I will be call-ed "whipped", or any name you can think of. I will be called a punk. But, I proved who a real punk is, a feminine mind, (I can see it now, the "church" is going to come out of me, I am still trying not to go there).

By the way, remember, boys call names, boys hurt people. Real men do not. Real men can talk things through. Boys are violent (unnecessarily), I will say.

Call me names; prove how positive I am with your negative. (sorry ladies, back to the matter at hand).

When a man pays he is showing he not only cares, but he understands life and nature, and maybe spirit, (but this is a later discussion). He knows how to be a man. Lets face it. Naturally, a paying man doesn't seem to mean he's a real man, but ladies; you know, something deep within lets you know that something is very right about this.

Even if I can't explain it fully (you see it's a spiritual thing). God is a spirit, it's a closer to God way for a man, than not: don't you think? Don't you sense what I am trying to show you wonderful women?

Breadwinners, payers, givers, isn't their something manly about him being different. You must see what I am showing you.

(What if he doesn't have money)? Good question. Why go on a date? Well, I'll be bold and say that no one should date.

Now is the author, changing the subject, oh no. I just am very ready to apply all my positive-truth knowledge to you ladies; I don't know what to do. Oh, dating you say, glad you mentioned it, read next chapter, (and you thought this ruffled-feathers)!

Chapters 3

Dating

I know that it seems I have been coming out with blatant statements that do not seem to match reality. But reality is not real. Yes I'm unreal. I'm crazy; whatever you call this "real man".

But, back to the subject, don't you ladies agree with this paying "stuff"? If you do, it's not because you are ladies, but it's because it's the truth coming out and touching the truth in you. Guys have truth too; it's just buried under muscle false-pride and arrogance, sometimes.

Well, I'm back to it again, from the spirit-world with another one: dating is evil, dating is a lie, dating is overrated. Dating is like religion. It says "look at me do so good right now". Dating is a trap.

Throw out this word dating. You don't need it. It's pressure, it's like pressing fast-forward on a good slow-developing love story; and the tape pops. Why call it a date? Change your thinking.

I must let you know, I am not bitter, I am not hurt, even some of you ladies might think something is wrong with me. It is not. I am not angry with guys, I am one. (I am just making sure we see eye to eye).

Dating is the "fakest" piece of garbage out there. I will tell you this: dating is another bad sign of future shakiness. Just go out with the guy as "a friend". You do not have to rush off anywhere.

I know dating seems normal, guess what? It is; and so is cheating. But, why go through it. Just because everyone is dating or cheating or eating fast food, doesn't make it right or healthy.

When I first met my wife, I never dated her (right away). I admit I am different, but in my "different-ness", I can show you something. I met her unintentionally, but we talked for about an hour that day, in March 93.

I did not "see her" until 5 months later. I am not saying you have to follow this exactly. Even though I didn't see her for 5 months, we talked nearly everyday. 5 months after that was the next time I had seen her again. We still talked daily.

I really got to know her (and no there was no one else). So now we are talking August 93 and then January 94. After this was June 94.

I broke the cycle when I saw her the next month. This was July. Late that month things started to heat.

But, I already got to know her. Yes I'll admit we both thought of more than talk. Honestly, it became more than talks by Fall.

So once again, I'll interpret the happenings in my life for good, or for a lesson. I do believe if I had even seen my (now) wife more often, I would not have gotten to know her correctly, only too soon, erectly: which I thought I didn't mind. I had it in mind to wait (you know), but we failed at our goal. A good foundation was laid though. This foundation was not because of sex. It did take over things though, but we kept growing together in other ways too.

Some would now call me a hypocrite, I would not argue, but I'm over this stage and we are married now.

I apologized to God, and I felt guilty, but I cared for her then (I know it does not make it right). I am thankful I turned out okay. Now can't you see that there is something different in me?

You see, I tried a goal, of waiting to marriage, and my then "friend" refused to let me go all the way without "dating" her, so I did date her. I did try to have sex without commitment, first. But, our seeing each other every 5 months helped save us. Even I tried to use her, yes I did.

So ladies, the next matter is when.

Well, to be honest, I must say wait to marriage. I have to have that in writing. I cannot go against the scriptures, in good conscience. I didn't wait exactly, but my goal was nearly successful, until I saw her a month apart.

If the temptation is there to have sex, and you don't love him (I should say), if he doesn't love you, it is a very bad sign: of future cheating.

Some people might say I really am a hypocrite, but think carefully, I am wanting the best for you, as a precaution. I know it's easier for me to say; but if you can't wait until marriage, I cannot say give it half a year, (but I'll think it for you).

Please let this man get to know you. It shouldn't be that you are waiting six months, in suffering hard temptation (I'm just thinking six months should only be talking and growing together). Stay away from thinking of each other in that way. Talk on the phone, just don't "date". Go to your rooms and talk over the phone. I know you say this is childish; so is a blueprint of a building on paper. But look how serious-of-a-building can be plainly built; (and by the way, I waited 22 years, let that give you strength); (and I waited 17 months after I first seen, who I now, am married too).

You can do it, no excuses. If you are active, please (I won't say stop), but, please make ways to avoid, and avoid and avoid sex until you two get to truly know each other. (Then prove your knowledge and love of each other by marriage).

If you are a virgin, oh my God, God bless you, please wait until marriage, I personally love you and look up to you in your strength. You are a real special person. I felt ashamed as a virgin, but I tell you now, do not be ashamed. If you happened to know a guy virgin; this is about the most wonderful and greatest, most positive sign of a man, a real man that doesn't and will not cheat (once in a relationship).

A virgin these days, to me is one of the greatest characteristics in a human that I can think of. I admit, they are more wonderful than I was and am. I personally give them top credit.

God bless all you virgins, you are role models, indeed. Do not listen to anyone say, "you do not know what you are missing" You are not missing anything.

You are guaranteeing yourself a wonderful relationship. (I can't say enough).

This book doesn't even compare to you. You are this book's hope. Learn your future spouse. If you are "seeing someone" keep learning and talk honestly, and not about sex, (especially between the two of you-in actual action; if all possible).

Do not listen to that lie of "see if it fits", the world always has something to say. Do not buy into it all. Remember, the world is boastful and yet sad and miserable. Whatever name you are called, soak it up. Stay with your head up, and panties and pants up.

Once you get married, you would be more that glad you did it, and most of the people who ridiculed you will be dead, sick or just plain unhappy. So you stay happy.

(People who sleep-around are not happy). You can't do things your way and be happy. God is happiness and He created it, and we must do things His way; not by force, but because we want too.

"Little Keisha, don't touch the stove". Why did the mother say this? - was it to be mean? -no. To be controlling? -no. Is it because she doesn't like little Keisha? -no.

Little Keisha has to learn "how and when to work" a stove. A stove is not a bad thing, neither is sex, but anyone can touch it. Some get burned, some die, some put on gloves (which will get burned later, by being so cautious and other things go wrong; some wait until the stove is cooled down (getting to know someone) and then touch (in marriage).

Chapter 4

What are you Wearing

I may have been hard on the men. This was not my intent. I may have been unreal about dating, but it's real tragic how women cannot see how it destroys relationships.

Well ladies, you have to ride through the truth-storm you must now face.

What are you wearing? You know what you are wearing. You know what you are doing.

There are many types of wearing. What clothes are you wearing? What mind state are you wearing? Are you wearing out your body?

Suggestive clothes, or the lack of clothes, are all I see on women. Yes it is tempting to most men, and it can make a real man sad. He knows you can do better.

I know you heard it all before. "I can wear what I want", "Honey-girl how I look", or "what are you looking at."

This is all a world of worldly-hell. You say how can dressing a certain way be hell. Well, all women who dress revealing are in a mental hell. I mean, they are not burning or anything. They live in a confused, contradicting and sorry state. They think dressing revealing can help them find a man.

Dressing like that will only help them find just that, a man, not a real man. A man that cares only for sex. (I know you know this already), (let me step it up, I know mostly ladies will be reading this but I must deliver with tough-love). Ladies you are being nothing but whorish, dressing like this, good for nothing but sexing (to be polite). You know what you are doing. Collect and cover yourselves.

You are so hurt by some man, that you think you can rush the job of finding another one. Maybe your daddy didn't love you or hug you enough, maybe you had no-daddy. Well, let me open you up properly. God loves you and He is masculine. This is all the masculine you need, or you should need to help heal your mind.

I know in this state, of you dressing like a whore, it's hard to change, but you have to. Maybe you don't feel sexy enough. Don't you notice, when you dress like this, you still are not happy. You keep on trying to get attention, and you probably think you look better than other women. Well, you do not.

I don't and wouldn't want you like that. No real man would. You may feel like you are the sexy-one around town, but you are not.

If you want to continue to be on guard, or hurt, or stay in a "bad relationship", it's your fault. Bad relationship -meaning potentially attracting a bad relationship, in this case.

To see a woman in such tight revealing clothes, any man can't take you serious, and only the bad ones would make a move. Dressing like this is evil. (Meaning that it is not of God or Godly). It is like you are used toilet tissue, an-every-bodies-been-there kind of woman; like some fake diamond, cheap that can be bought by anyone. Wow, you impress me not. Cover yourself.

When a woman is covered, she has respect, and believe it or not she is happier. You might not feel happy at first, if you are not used to being covered. But believe me, happiness will come soon.

When you cover, you might feel unworthy, or like that "other woman" is getting all the attention. Believe me, you are the special one. You are that real pure diamond, no one can afford. Be patient. You are the one who is truly attractive. You will live in peace and a mental-pain-free relationship will come your way.

The wonderful and wholesomeness of your covering is beyond obvious beauty. Obvious beauty dies quickly.

Real beauty lasts long and is truly revealed at night (at least in private, it should be).

Very few people can understand the beauty of a covered woman. Any uncovered woman should be for her spouse eyes to see.

When a woman can be eyed up and down without imagination, that's a dead woman, and nothing comes forth except her butt, her breasts, her butt, her "position" in a mans head, her butt and her butt. Her head is nowhere in sight. Her face doesn't really matter: and you can throw her feelings out of the window. (Dead woman -meaning dead as in attracting flies; flies go around dead things-think).

God is not impressed, and neither am I. Anything negative or evil only satisfies a little while. Hint: that's how long your relationship (which is in false quality will last; little, and painful while it lasts).

If you want a faithful man, be faithful to yourself.

If a man really loves you he would not want to see you near-naked or too revealing, in public; another sign of a real man. He wouldn't want anyone to see you sexually-dressed.

Hint: would he want to see his mother or sister like that? Not even a halfway decent man would want to see that. He shouldn't love you like a mother or sister, but believe me this love is similar.

(A real man will care even about your nose and your toes, not just your holes and your being exposed).

(A real man will care even about your period, not just where his Trojan is).

Do you get it, your being loved should be tender, not only a bender.

Chapter 5

Communication

What are you talking about? Everyone talks about communication in a relationship, and how important it is. I will be communicating to you about real communication.

First of all, I writing to you now is communication. Communication is the fertilization of two people's minds, (if communication is done with real quality).

When I write, like I said before, I write from my heart, not my mind. The only time I use my mind is to decide on controlling what in my heart I should write, and how I write. What I mean is, I write the truth, and I have no hidden agendas. (No hidden agendas means: my agenda is not hidden, because by now I hope you understand it; if not now, you will soon.

This book is for me and my family, and for support towards relationships and it is against cheating; (an offense I take very seriously and I think deserves "jail time". Wow, did I mean that, well, yes-no and yes. The "no" is so you won't think I'm crazy, you be the judge. How much does no-cheating mean to you?

We really have to take cheating seriously, so this is how and why I communicate.

You see, I wear my heart on my sleeve, once you get to know me. I do act in a "fake way" in the past and still on occasions. What I mean is this: By me not speaking on or telling anyone how bad cheating is, means I was acting "fake".

It seems cool and acceptable to hear about cheating, right. It's just, "opps I cheated" or "he cheated on her" or "he has been cheating on her". These news flashes are no longer okay. I have a heart for relationships that are faithful. I feel relationships, so now I speak, in writing. This book will back me up. God created relationships, He created the who, how, and why-together in them.

Speaking of "back me up" what about "back that thang up". Is this okay to you? What are you talking about with your friends? Do you take it seriously, these songs?

Well, you should, if you want a good relationship, or to keep a good relationship. (Another note from that spirit world -there is no such thing as a good relationship. What do I mean? Well, relationships are good; you don't need to specify that it's good; this is redundant. There is "relationships", "bad relationships", and horrible relationships". It is these add-on words that kill relationships).

A relationship is a good thing, if you don't do good or communicate, it is bad.

Do not bother living in fear or doubt, because this cannot help a relationship. You need to communicate (with real communication).

The world thinks communication is talking. Some smart people think it's talking and hearing. Some geniuses think it's talking and listening (oh they are so smart, they didn't just hear, they listened).

I will tell you that they are not wrong, but are "brittily" correct. They are correct, but in their correctness, their knowledge cannot help them, in the very long run. (Not into short-term relationships, or short term anything).

Communicating is talking, hearing, and listening to everything good and bad. Whether it is involved in the relationship or not. What I mean is, a couple must weigh what they hear (on the outside), and what to let into the relationship. Check if what they hear is good or bad: if it's good or bad to self or to the partner.

Communication must cover all aspects of life (with proportion to the time involved, in the relationship). Eventually, "after a few months, 6 or more"- all thoughts, feeling, and knowledge about each other should be on the table.

It may seem difficult to do this, but real relationships take time to start. That's why I feel more confident talking and telling you to get to know each other over months time, without any kind of sexual-talking, which leads to greater chances of cheating in the future.

Sex too early, in these days may seem normal, but like falling out of a 10 story building into a big tree: you still most likely will die -and he most likely will cheat.

The relationship may break-up. I know it sounds "high school" and childish, but I am pro-relationship, this is what it takes. Pain is not childish, and don't think you would not want to be a child again if you get hurt bad enough.

Innocence is always looked down on as ignorance, in this day and age. A child is innocent, and your relationship should be too, like a child.

A little child tells his or her "mommy" anything, positive or negative. Truth events are spoken on, to their "mommy". A couple should be similar. Here is an example of telling it all, no matter how small or insignificant it is. Remember, it's insignificant to the degree of us all being brainwashed and living in "acceptation" of things we hear, see and understand.

Example: The man comes by, and he is your boyfriend. -"hey baby", -kiss-, "how are you doing?" Girlfriend- "fine, how are you?" Boyfriend-"I'm okay, that girl "so-and-so" had on those tight shorts, down the block, again." Girlfriend"-oh, well don't worry about that."

Now see, this is the silliest example, isn't it. It seems so insignificant, even make-believe. But, let me explain. This is how a real man should communicate. Naturally he knows the sight of this woman is tempting, (temptation is not a bad thing -it's what you do, after), and he will be thinking of this image as he is telling her (you).

To you, (her) it may not be a big thing, and it's not, but it's a real thing. It was not the first time he seen her in anything tight, but by him expressing (communicating), the temptation goes away.

Thoughts start small, we all know that, so make sure you talk and he talks about all things, big and small. Even if it is repetitive situations. (A relationship is not automatic; it has to be kept up. Just as you bathe daily, it must be "bathed" in communication") daily.

All activities should be done together. If it is not possible, at times, like shopping or work, etc. It should at least be talked about. What happened, what did you buy, who did you see, where did you go, etc.

Learn to be fond of one another. "What's going on, are you okay, who, what, when, where, did, should, could, would, won't, will, if, and next time."

The world is a war, and communicating is a great weapon to fight all forms of negativity; by friends, News, rumors, statistics, "negative-trues", "true-lies", and things that cause doubt, pain, fear, or sayings of "trust-me".

Remember a couple is a hated thing, by the world's standards. What do I mean? The world may not say they hate you, but, relationships are expected to fail. There are expectations of mistrust, lying, or the acceptance of the future "fact-saying" of "all men cheat", or, "he's going to cheat".

(I must say, when I am writing this book, do not think that I am bitter at a woman that hurt me, no one hurt me. Do not think that I have something against men, I do not. I'll say it again; I am pro-relationship. Pro, pro, pro, so understand those things).

If you think that a man will cheat, he will. If you think he might not cheat, then he will "might-not cheat."

There should be no such thing as "thinking" a man will not cheat. You cannot think this, you have to know this.

It's like building a building; you know it will not fall. (Remember, we are in a negatively-vibed world); now didn't the thought of "but buildings have fallen", cross your mind. This thinking is from a negative spirit-world. I said negative this time, as opposed to positive. (Remember, I'll explain explicitly, what I mean). (If I explained already -some readers would label this book a religious book. Remember, religion scares, and or intimidates most people. I am not religious; and do not think I am against "the big-guy" upstairs).

Knowing your man should be like knowing gravity, (if the "building-example" is not your flavor). Gravity is reliable. If you throw up a rock, it will come back down, because of gravity.

Real communication [(pure, repetitive, simple, totally given talks, pre-cautionary talks, and even secrets (in month's time) can and should be discussed)].

Communicate up, not down. Communicate in spite of. What I mean is this: Have you heard the saying "two people should be complete without each other"- this statement is a lie, and a half. By communicating in spite of: you two-together should know and say -you complete me. (Not right away, should this be said, or even be the case -but it will come in month's time).

The world wants you to think two people should be complete when starting out, that way they will think you don't have to need each other; if so-called trouble comes.

Yes you should be complete, individually in some ways, but a partner does some completion too. They complete spiritually, mindfully, and then (after months), physically (best in marriage).

Communication over months is a spiritual marriage, but no excuses, get married on paper. What is so evil about marriage? What? Nothing, if the foundation is right.

(Another spiritual truth from that "spiritual world"-people do not have sex in the foundation of a house, they have sex in the house. So slowly built your foundation right. A foundation is made mostly of communication, full communication.

Expect his call, nothing wrong with that, expect to know where he is at all times. What's wrong with that? He should want to know where you are too. He should expect your call.

Do not think these things are foolish, impossible, difficult or annoying. Remember, it is you who wants to get a man that doesn't cheat. These things are part of how. Remember, gravity, remember my saying of "months", and months without (destroying your young-foundation half done), you know what I am trying to say. No letting him in the "door" (of your foundation). Foundations support vertical things, things that stand, stay "vertical". If you "horizontalize (have sex)" in your foundation, your foundation will "horizontalize (fall)" on you, and you would have "rubble (trouble, future betrayal)" etc.

So resist the common theme, about "relationship-mental" beliefs. "Yeah I met this guy", "he seems nice", "he has money, and a nice car". "He buys me things".

Please do not use a man for things. You are only hurting yourself. It says a lot about you, doesn't it? Let other women do it, don't be like them. What goes around comes around.

Everything in life is spiritually lead by good or evil. I used the word evil many times to show you how serious life and relationships are. Be a good woman, and good things will come your way. Keep being all right, no matter who seems to get away with bad, no matter who seems to have fun, being proud and boastful. Yes, woman act up too; be yourself, be anew, and if you are acting in an ill manner; change now, (by practicing right).

(You will get what you "act" for).

Chapter 6

That Spiritual World

Hello, you have arrived to where I hope you'd come to. I am glad you kept reading, thus far. Love yourself right now please, really love yourself and be proud of yourself in the right way.

Once again, I am not religious, and I do not think "I" know anything. I would like you to understand a world (not this one) that I try to stay in spiritually and mentally.

I want to now, truly communicate with you (no holding back now).

Women are usually more open than men. I am an open man. (Open -to honesty and spirituality).

A man who is open to his woman or to God; the world (the regular people world), always has something bad to say about it.

I get my ways from the spirit-world. It came through my parents (especially father), molding me in real manly things.

To get a real man, first of all the world would not think this is real, because they cannot "see" him. Real men don't cheat and real men are spiritual.

Spiritual men are nearly always acting properly. Natural men are nearly always acting improperly.

To a natural man, spiritual things do not exist. He or she sees what they see, (which is the negative), in the world, and that's it. There is the belief that "everyone cheats", or "everyone cheats sometimes"; or even "everyone cheats once" fine, believe that, accept that, and you will get that.

A natural person sees a spiritual person as different, (they are different). A spiritual person does not have to have a holy sign or halo on his or her head. People can tell whose opposite them, "deep inside". This is some of that spiritualism we all have.

You see, even a natural person, (usually walking negatively, thinking negative, and accepting negativity) is spiritual. What I mean is; that person's spirituality is unknown to that person.

This spirituality is a negative spirituality that forces you to walk "naturally".

Walking naturally means to walk "normally", and, that person thinks normally. Is normal bad?

Well, "normally" has its limits, (it's very limited). Walking normally is (along with thinking normally) ;(and since we are speaking on relationships), says: "all cheat", "all men are dogs", etc.

See, the weird thing is (now open your mind), they are absolutely correct. In the natural, all men do cheat. It is the normal thing to do. Get it. Normal used to be good, but now normal is like the number zero next to a negative number. (It offers nothing positive). If you add the zero (representing doubt, fear, what's going on in the world, "everybody's doing it phrases", etc.); you end up still negative. If you multiply the zero with a negative number you still have nothing.

Negative spirituality keeps you down, confused, fearful, doubtful, stubborn, proud, and it seals deep in your mind that everything you do is right. It tells you everyone is wrong, especially those who are "truly" right. It has you not to listen to them. It tells you they are crazy, or boring, or that those positive situations are not real. Everything is cynical. It keeps you feeling hopeless, angry, unforgiving and even suicidal: (can anyone say -demoniacally lead).

See, when you are controlled by negative -spiritualism, it is not considered spirituality. "Spirituality" is known to only be in so-called church. Church is fine as long as it has "that" correct "spirituality" (I'll get to).

A man killing his family, or a woman killing her kids, (this is negative spirituality. These people are actually "normal" in their eyes. At the moment of acting, they were not wrong (to themselves).

This spiritually makes you do evil things, bad things, "cool things", wasteful things, and most of the time "no-thing (laziness)". (A battle I admit fighting, still), (and writing this book is "doing something to personally help that); (people out in the world need my help), (I'm good for something, and I now act; but back to the book:)

People can easily see faults in others, like the man or woman killing their family, but I'll tell you that every act that is not beneficial is ungodly. Whether it hurts you or someone or some situation.

Stealing, lying, manipulating, even lusting, smoking, and fornicating. In these things, they hurt someone, or hurt self, or even hurt God (His feelings -and yes, He has feelings) and these things ultimately destroy you anyway.

See, doing some things are negative, and we don't see it that way, or maybe we don't care: being that it doesn't harm us "physically", right away.

It is not that I want to go on a spiritual tantrum; I want you to recognize all sides of negative spirituality- not necessarily negative to us (at the time).

The person, killing is "so-bad", but we can be too. Being positively spiritual, [(actually simply put - being spiritual, (as oppose to natural (normal), (fleshy), (regular)], is seeing and understanding self and when self does wrong, then recognizing the world and others, (to help them): when they do wrong.

All this relates to the book, (when choosing a real man). You must be lead spiritually to know it is definitely possible to get a man that does not cheat.

It is not good enough to just know yourself, but to know about the spirit, to know yourself spiritually.

(No human being is good or evil). They are lead by a positive spirit (Godly), or a negative spirit (ungodly). A positively lead person is "spiritual", a negatively lead person is natural, normal, "in the flesh", "logical".

What's wrong with logic, you ask? What's wrong with being normal? Again, there is nothing wrong, except this: example: Jane found out she has a terminal disease. Logical thinking is that she is going to die. Normal thinking is to listen to logic. "The doctor said so", "the charts say so", "I saw the x-rays myself", "I feel sick", etc.

Now this woman-going to die is "normal", (since we all will die), but; is it positive. No. That means it is negative, and if indeed negative; then it is bad. It is: even (evil). This dying is not of God, so it's ungodly. Believing she is going to die (from this disease), "is" ungodly. Why? A disease is not good, is it? no. It's evil, and thinking it is in charge is also evil. How can this disease control a human, "as to when they die or not"? ("Well God did it"-really, is that what you think. -no He did not).

43

Naturally, and natural thinking says, she is going to die "soon". But, if you are spiritual; you can understand that "Jane" does not have to die "soon". Be positively spiritual, because negatively spiritual is the same as normal, natural and "logical".

"But I am spiritual, God is calling her, I believe in God, see". -this is a lie, too. Why does God need a disease to so-call call someone. Just keep blaming God for everything -this is not right.

It is a fact, she will die soon, it's real; but step in faith to the positive thinking spiritual world. You see, the negative spirit-world is automatic thinking; it takes effort to positively believe beyond normal thinking.

Well, what could she do? I am glad you asked. Now here comes the rated-R (what they might call religious writing), or even (I can say); here comes rated-X (from what I will call explicit "non-politically correct", "crazy talk"- controversial), etc., etc.

Remember you are in a negative, contaminated world (demons all around -I'm talking about they make you focus on "negative" normal thinking). This, what I'm about to say is not normal. You may think you know it, but I'm confident nearly all do not (the readers, that is).

All men will cheat, without God in them. -(since this book is about not cheating).

All men and women cannot get along, without God in them.

Women dressing overly sexy are being lead by evil, (and evil will happen to them. Why do I call it evil? Well, it's not good, that's why, and: this book is about not cheating; -she is fast-forwarding the process of getting a "normal" ungodly man, (who will cheat -this is the evil that will happen to her).

Let me break down God. Really having God. (Now if you really want a man that does not cheat, do not be afraid to read and understand what I'm about to write.

(I might be judged for so-call "preaching", but I'm not). (If you believe telling the truth is preaching -then I am). You figure this one out.

God is a spirit, and He is in the spiritual world. He is the truth. Truth -meaning, He is more than just a fact. Is a fact the truth? Not necessarily.

Remember "Jane", it is a fact that she is going to die soon, but the truth is (if she believed in God (truly), she could be healed. What do I mean truly?

Explicit content: warning: - (If a man or woman does not believe in God's Son), they do not "truly" believe in God (as far as God is concern). (Note: this is not my opinion). [(How dare you think I (the author) am so important)]? (I truly am nothing -I know this -it's what's "in" me that makes me) something.

Biblically speaking, God's Son is the only "way" to anything (life), (peace, money, health, healing, protection, and getting a faithful man). Do you really want a real good man?

(I am not trying to use this book to beat God over your head -so watch your thinking; remember where it can come from).

God's Son is called Jesus (He is a real man). He actually made the way to all that is good. He took our sins (you heard that before), and he took our diseases, fears, hopelessness, greed, doubt, cancers, etc.. He gives life, health, peace, bravery, protection, and can bring a good real non-cheating man in your life: (even correct a presently cheating man).

Jane can be healed. If she believes in Jesus' name, she is already healed in God's eyes. She must pray in His name. She has to believe this. This is "spirituality". This is illogical, this belief is not normal. This believing is the "truth"; (not the true-fact she would die, but the true truth that she would live).

The spirit controls the mind, and the mind controls the flesh (physical). God is a spirit, so when He said, "Let there be light", it was in his mind what He wanted. When He had spoken, then light showed up.

If I ask you to make a fist, you must think about doing it (the split-second) before you do it. This is your mind controlling your physical.

So if you want something good, in the flesh (the physical-daily world) you must go to the spiritual world (in faith), where God is; and accept in your mind; then the 3-dimensional world will respond. That is, getting healed, getting that job, and yes -getting your man (real man).

Getting a real good man is not hard. It is a process that takes time. You must be positive and fair and focused. Stand strong in faith.

Say what you want, and behave in all areas, as this book says; know what to look for, know what to listen to. Know when the devil is talking in your ear (through friends, "common acceptances" to normal situations", "News media", other "seemingly smart books", "he say she say", ungodly counsel", "logic", "doubt", "fear", low expectations", etc. Remember step up, step out and stay spiritual.

A lot of the things we do harm us spiritually. God loves us, but He will not force us to do what's right. Since we are dealing with relationships, we need a relationship with God, not religion.

Religion says, "I'll do this and that, then I'll be righteous". Relationship says, "we need God, and to know Him; we should know His word (the bible)". -But, how do we know that's Gods word"? -(What did I say about negative- thinking)? Just try the bible, and pray. Worry about church later. It's not church that saves you. Don't fake-out God. You might not be a churchgoer, or want to go now; but please read a "King James Version", bible. Be real; read John's Gospel, good stuff.

In the world (regular-thinking normal people), there are things that seem right, but they are only right to us, but not with God. Some of these things are our everyday or once in a while pleasures.

Now, to be Godly or ungodly is easy, just choose a side. One way will keep you; one way will eventually kill you. One will be peaceful, fear free, confident living. The other will be painful, fearful, doubtful; dying (living this way); (walking-dead, everything getting you "messed up" or kept down).

Do not be afraid of God or uncomfortable. He made us, where can you hide. If we do things His way, we will truly be happy; in spite of what the world does, says, and thinks.

A faithful man is possible, do not doubt, but remember; we must have Godly ways, to benefit. Our negativity-thinking or negative actions (whether they seem negative or not) must be rid from our lives.

(Sometimes we must rid our lives of something, because God says it's not Godly), (God knows best, and we must trust Him, even if we do not want to, or believe to).

Sometimes we have to have the knowledge of how He sees things, to see how bad things are.

Evil breeds evil, lying breeds lying, and fornication, breeds (opens the door to) massive cheating, adultery (once married), and more fornication and cheating. Read next chapter.

Chapter 7

Fornication

As I said in the last chapter, we must understand what God thinks. We have to see things Gods way. Fornication is the mother of cheating. Fornication is "cheating". Cheating, how?

God does not want us to fornicate. Is he just being controlling, or docs He have a reason, does He not care?

You see, our physical bodies do not belong to us (this is biblical), (not my opinion), they are His. He "loaned" them to us to be fruitful and multiply. Only our free-minds are ours. With our minds we make the choice to obey God or not. Whether we understand His ways or not.

You see, when you are spiritual, you have an open mind and you can receive "positive-knowledge". (I just learned something just now as I'm writing you).

I learned from the fact that in earlier chapters or a chapter, I wrote I hate cheating. I think I wrote this. Anyway. If I didn't write it (by my memory), I am thinking it.

What I learned is -why am I thinking I hate cheating, and fornication is cheating on God. I never even thought about writing that I hate fornication. Do you know why? It is because, naturally thinking, I was subconsciously thinking, " okay, cheating hurts -so it's bad; but fornication (when I did it, it felt so good), I didn't think it was bad "off the back".

You see, one has to stay thinking spiritual. All of my life, I never thought I hated fornication. "It was with the one I love", "I eventually married her", "it's with the same woman". You see (I was wrong) in my thinking. I knew cheating was wrong (enough to hate, immediately), but not fornication.

God loves us so much, that He can't stand us being with someone we do not love (in a marriage setting). We all may say, "you don't have to marry". Well, would you want a child-abuser with a child? Would you want a shark to eat a family member you love? Would you want to be raped?

The answers are no, because "you" either feel it's wrong, understand it's wrong, or know it's wrong.

Well, to the child-abuser: the child is there, so why not. With the shark, it's hungry; it's okay. With the rapist, he "feels" it's necessary, "he" wants it, and no one is looking: he goes for it. He is not being hurt, so he thinks, "who cares".

This is how God feels about us and fornication. It seems okay to us, but to him, it's like an act that hurts Him because we would be hurting ourselves; even though it feels so, oh-so pleasurable.

Why does it hurt God? Because it hurts us, it degrades the value of sex. "So what".

Well, this act is spiritually damaging because we most likely are not in-love with who we are with (at the time). "So what, how does it really hurt me"? Our bodies are sacred, and when we have sex with a person we are not married to, we are building so many curses around us. So many open gates of negative events can happen. "So, I'll use a condom". Condoms, if not used medically, are a deception.

Remember what I said, watch your thinking. These statements are what a non-spiritual person would sound like.

I personally, am trying to describe as best I can, how wrong fornication really is.

Some of the physical negative gates are, disease, sickness etc. Fornication can also hurt the mind. It brings shame (conscience or subconsciously), doubt and fear, and guilt. It even brings hopelessness. Why, what, how?

When you have many partners, you lose your heart, without knowing it. You are defiled, and you know you are not really happy.

God did not create us to fornicate. He doesn't create situations that bring shame, guilt and fear, and even unsatisfaction (long-term). -(short-term anything is usually evil).

Fornication cannot and never will, make you happy. Sex in marriage is so fulfilling. Yes there is always temptation, (temptation is just the devil talking). He is instigating the situation; he wants you to come into his world.

If fornication is okay, why do most people either (hide, use condoms, sneak-around, fear or are uncomfortable)? God wouldn't create situations like these.

Imagine it is normal to hide the "facts of your acts" (as an unmarried young person), or have to wear condoms. God didn't create a condom on or in a person. You are trying to force the situation of false-love. Why would God create sex and there's a "disease" out there you have to watch for, around it? Why are people who fornicate, really not taking their time, and sweating together? Why are the clothes, half way off? Why are the lights out? Where's the communicating, where's the long term planning.

All of these things are ungodly "uncomfortable-fearful-shameful occurrences". So much work, so little fun. What good is a "quickie"?

Women, you do not need this, you are not built for this. "What about the men?" The focus is you now (this is your book, to help correct your thinking on how to truly "get some").

You know you are truly happy (long-run happy), when you have one good man, who loves you, and can talk mouth-to-mouth, not only "south-to-south". You know, you are trying so hard to make like you are happy, when you don't "do it" Gods wonderful way.

Happiness depends on real righteous situations. Unrighteous situations bring unhappiness. There is not one truly happy fornicating woman on earth. If a woman can get as wild as a guy (and I'm not being scxist), this is really bad. There is a 100% chance she is not happy.

Happiness is something the world tries to grab, but cannot. Women who are unhappy dress revealing. The more unhappy, the more revealing, (whether you know or not).

A sexy woman in public is not happy. She is seeking, for attention. Lady, you do not have to do this. I said it before; let other women dress this way. You stay humble. Your real man will come.

(God made a man, so in "Godliness" will you get a real one, not "your way"). (A diamond is special because no one can hardly afford it). (A diamond is a hard substance, so you please play hard to get); and just watch how you shine.

(A natural man is "blind", he cannot "see" spiritual things, and he can only "feel"), and he "feels" he wants you in bed. Get to know a good man, from the start. Stop the sexy-hook, you only hook trouble. -(Flies come around garbage). Public sexiness is shallow overrated garbage. Sensuality cannot mix with spirituality, never. You need spiritual beginnings, and then sensual (long term) endings.

Chapter 8

Closing

I really hoped this book was a great help. I believe you now have the choice to get the man you need.

I am not fancy, or have great "parting words"; being non-politically correct (by my honesty), I know that I am still what I am, because of the Holy Spirit.

He is that voice of positivity in your ear. He is the Spirit of Truth (biblical). He is the real power behind why I have not, will not, and do not want to cheat on my wife.

I can say how wonderful my wife is, but I say that by my actions. My actions are choices (from within) that I keep in. Remember, God doesn't force anyone to do right.

We all do wrong, sometimes, and at least think of doing wrong. But we must rely on the Holy Spirit to remind us to behave, and get in our minds so deep, we actually want to do right.

I really find it disgusting to even think about cheating on my wife. This does not make me good. If I thought that not cheating makes me good, then I am religious-and self-righteous.

If you have a real man, already: let me at least say something about something.

Christianity keeps my marriage. By God who saved me with His Son Jesus, and when Jesus died and went back to heaven, once he had come here; He sent the Holy Spirit. If you don't like God, or know anything about Him, just believe he loves and loved, and will always love you. That's why His gift is Jesus. I am saved, and righteous (only because I believe in Jesus), not because I'm so-called good. I can be good without Him, or bad without Him; all in all it's "still bad" without Him".

The Holy Spirit (the 3rd person of God), teaches me truth and teaches me about what is a lie, and unknown truth.

(If you go in a room filled with balloons, and some float, and others don't; do not think these balloons who float are special. These are filled with helium as opposed to being filled with air). Religion is air, other theories are air, but Christianity and God, Jesus, and the Holy Spirit are that helium. I am filled "with the spirit", that's why I (the author) am a man that doesn't cheat. Many church-goers still cheat, it's not the church, it's not the sexy dressing or suits or robes, or even the long dresses, it's the Spirit (Holy Spirit).

(How to get a man that doesn't cheat, get him in Jesus, and filled with the Spirit), but you first. (Water, ice, and vapor are all H^{2}O). (God the Father, God the Son (Jesus), and God the Holy Spirit, are all God, and that faithful man can be all yours).

.

About the Author

A married man of almost 9 years, and has two children. Raised as a Christian, whose values have been learned by seeing knowledge and wisdom acted out. Though a Christian, was taught values (without church-like Christian) teaching. Teaching came from the spiritual-world, not man-made "Christian Doctrine."

Mr. Charles E. Hughes, Jr.
e-mail addr. y32493@aol.com

Printed in the United States
40193LVS00001B/151-168